Robert Murase

Stone and Water

S P A C E M A K E R   P R E S S

Text by Michael Leccese

Washington DC

Cambridge MA

Front cover: Private Residence
Photo by Robert Murase

Publisher: James G. Trulove
Spacemaker Press

Designer:
Sarah Vance

Editor:
D. Sperry Finlayson

Production Coordinator:
Susan McNally

Printer:
Tien Wah Press, Singapore

ISBN 1-888931-03-5

Acknowledgments

The projects illustrated in this book are
a reflection of a dedicated staff, those
individuals both past and present whose
collaboration, technical expertise, pa-
tience, and perseverance have been an
invaluable asset to me.

It is impossible to acknowledge by
name all of the individuals—clients,
teachers, architects, artists, landscape
architects, designers, craftsmen, and
stonemasons—whose friendship I have
enjoyed, who have been an inspiration
and who have helped realize these
projects.

I would like to thank the publisher,
James Trulove; Michael Leccese for the
ability to translate my philosophy and
thoughts into words; Sarah Vance for
the superb layout work; Dodie Finlayson
for her editorial expertise; and my son,
Scott, who collected the photographs
and took some fine shots. Lastly, I am
indebted to Peter Walker, whose encour-
agement and fine example made this
book possible.

Contents

Nichibei no bunkaga niou

bara no machi.

"The culture of Japan/America

can be felt in the city of roses."

"The positioning of stone in the landscape is an ancient and sacred tradition and has always interested me—from the stone walls and megaliths in Europe—to stone gardens in Japan.

What attracts me to Japanese gardens lies in the essence of quietness which they express; their meditative emptiness, the illusion of nature, the effects of shadow and filtered light, and their stark simplicity. These gardens provide a keen sense of "wabi," the absence of any ostentatious element, and a sense of humility and melancholy. There is a dark, mysterious quality about them, an undiscoverable unknown which goes beyond our individual small self, which could be described as "yugen" in Japanese.

These are some of the qualities I strive to express in the design process. We measure the various elements of the landscape and use sketches and computer-aided drawings to communicate ideas and construction format. But these construction drawings cannot fully explain the qualities of touch or feeling that I want to instill in the organic nature and flow of the land, the primordial sense of an arrangement of stones being lifted and fractured from the earth, or of how the water should flow over a stone escarpment. That intuitive touch must be brought to the project on the site, improvised there, and communicated directly to the landscape contractors and stonemasons. Our construction drawings are precise where we can measure things with confidence, and abstracted and flexible to allow for site design opportunities.

As we build with stones to mark places, channel water and build walls and terraces, there is always a sense of anticipation and possible surprise. Like a potter who fires his pots in a "nobori-gama," a wood-fired kiln, the artist who works in the landscape with stone and water cannot be sure of exactly what the final result will be; it is not something that can be entirely controlled. In the making of pottery, temperature variation, the action of fire and ash, and a host of variables alter and form the work. I anticipate and treasure the same kind of unexpected features as they affect and enrich the work in our practice. We all contribute, but when water moves over or between stones, it follows its own course. The final quest for beauty is given to us from a greater earth power. We can only make right our heart."

R.K.M.

Robert Murase

by Michael Leccese

Early on a June morning in Portland, Oregon, Robert Murase enters the "model room" in his walk-up studio. Although the Northwest skies are pewter grey, and ivy grows over the windows, light floods the huge room in the former anchor rope factory. The neighborhood, the Pearl District, has been changing lately from industrial to fashionable. Across the street, welding sparks still fly at the Gender Machine Works, but a brewpub now shares the brick building where Murase's eighteen member firm has worked for nine years. The model room—the place where scale models of the firm's projects are produced—smells richly from hops stored one flight down.

Murase's son, Scott, is finishing a styrofoam mock-up of a proposed plaza. The model must be ready for presentation the next day to the client's board of directors in Los Angeles. The design incorporates patterns often found in Murase's work. Rectilinear pavings embrace a central section where the stones seem to have been pieced back together after an explosion. Chaos intrudes but is contained by order.

Scott holds up the model for his father's inspection. The elder Murase is a compact man who is generally reticent, and so soft-spoken that he can barely be heard over the traffic outside his office. On this occasion, however, he offers a blunt criticism. Spotting a blue seam that is not supposed to be visible, he makes an impatient gesture. "This is *not* good," he says abruptly. "This is not good."

Although Murase (pronounced mew-RAH-say) has designed many courtyards, plazas and gardens with intricate planting schemes, his favorite material is clearly stone, and his pursuit of perfection in this medium is legendary. "Things have to be done exactly," notes his friend and frequent collaborator, stonemason Edward Lockett of Vancouver, Washington. "If he wants four inches revealed on the stone, that doesn't mean five or six or three inches." When leading visitors through his own completed works, Murase may occasionally seem to completely forget the tour, wandering into planting beds pulling weeds or rearranging stones. Not one of those landscape architects who are seldom seen at the site after construction drawings have been conveyed to the contractor, Murase works closely with crews of five to eight masons, visiting job sites daily so he can improvise changes. "At the end of the day, we could be heading home and he'll start picking up pebbles and moving them around," says Lockett.

Murase's perfectionism can be easily accepted because his best work often approaches the flawlessness he seeks. In 1989, Seattle architect Richard Cardwell told *Landscape Architecture* magazine that Murase "places stones better than anyone, short of God himself. You'd swear those stones had always been there." [2] This innate skill is one source of his ability to infuse workaday modern places such as corporate campuses with a power and mystery that engage people on an archetypal level, but that they also find somehow soothing. It is a skill that has been honed by Murase's many hours of study in Japanese gardens, coupled with the good landscape architect's cinematic sense of how people move through and occupy space.

Paul Schell, a commissioner for the Port of Seattle, praises the way Murase's 750-foot-long Pier 69 Atrium on that city's waterfront works on so many levels. The exquisitely paved interior space is a symbol of the Port, a relaxing backdrop for the offices of 325 employees that open directly on to the Atrium, a place to receive foreign officials, and perhaps Seattle's most dignified and well-used indoor space for formal events. When children are present, they sail toy boats in the long, narrow "stream" that emerges first in feathered sheets from a stone pedestal. "It can be a stage for Japanese drummers or a playground for kids during events," says Schell. "It's a Zen garden with Northwest expression—very much 'out there' as an approach to landscape, yet it's not perceived as radical by the people who use it."

For all its technical precision, Murase's work often brings to mind monuments built by indigenous cultures. He frequently describes his projects as "neolithic" or "primordial." Yet they recall no particular place; they are not replicas of Easter Island monoliths or Egyptian obelisks. By including rough, field-collected stones, dry-stacked walls, and standing boulders, he seeks to elicit reverie rather than fantasy. "We speak of ancient forests and archaeological digs with deep reverence," he says, "but our culture has no sense of the spiritual or of symbols." Although Murase does not presume to fill that void, other observers recognize the connection. "There is a sense of entering ancient ceremonial chambers," wrote architecture critic Mark Hinshaw of the Pier 69 Atrium. "Murase has created in this progression of water and stonework a magnificent sense of serenity. Though people can be seen all around, the space seems private and contemplative." [3]

Influenced by enthusiasms as disparate as jazz music and the ceramic traditions of Japan, Murase recognizes that rather than stifling his ability to follow impulse, technical mastery enhances his freedom to act intuitively. Well-laid stone, he believes, shares virtues with the music he admires—a dynamic, spontaneous melody laid over syncopated rhythms. "It all goes by feel," he says. "Miles Davis once said to Herbie Hancock, 'You have a nice touch.' So much of it is an intuitive judgment that balances the feeling of the whole composition of stones. A lot of *shakuhachi* music (the plaintive song of the Japanese bamboo flute) is improvised. It's a matter of *feeling*."

When following an inner imperative, Murase will not hesitate to tinker with an installation that is ninety percent complete. One recent project, a large corporate facility, involved building a stream with waterfalls. "The working drawings had all stones standing straight up," he recalls. "But, after some reflection, I thought it would be more exciting to angle them. The client's representatives had some reservations, but after I explained the dynamics of vertical rhythms and geologic formations with the water coming over them, they agreed to the idea. By making it appear less stable, it becomes more exciting."

Murase's landscapes materialize slowly, like sculpture, from tons of boulders and quarried stones. His projects are painstakingly amassed, using cranes and front-end loaders, as well as ropes and pry bars. ("If you're watching, you might think it's a pretty crude process," says Lockett.)

Although he will use sandstone, he prefers harder, more durable stones such as granite, which is not found in Oregon, and basalt, the state's native igneous rock. When selecting stone, he seeks particular colors and sizes first, but often makes intuitive choices. During one memorable visit to a granite quarry in Cold Springs, Minnesota, Murase spotted the tip of a boulder emerging from the earth. He insisted that it be excavated. A twenty-seven-ton, almost perfectly round rock was taken from the spot where it had been deposited by glaciers. He named it the "mother stone." "I imagined it being tumbled in the ice age and made round and smooth," he says. He had a single hole drilled through the stone, which measures twelve feet high and eight feet wide. It was set at the top of a slope as the apparent source of a man-made stream.

Though his work is often too complex to be called minimalist, Murase can employ a minute gesture such as this drilling of a single hole in a huge boulder to great effect. He says, "Just building a simple stone wall, with a drainage swale next to it, is a powerful element. It's nothing more than that, but kids can play in the water, sit on the wall, walk along the path that marks the edge. These simple human elements added to the landscape make it engaging."

The idea is illustrated by a trio of low sculptures, made by Murase, that sit on the wooden floor of his studio. These pieces consist of large, angular shards of black granite he salvaged from the quarries at Cold Springs, Minnesota. Sometimes polished on one side, but with rough edges and drill marks exposed, the discarded stones are barely altered—except for a shallow, bowl-sized depression carved into one spot and filled with an inch or so of water, in which drifts a leaf or a petal from an office flower arrangement. These are perhaps variations on *tsukubai*-hollowed stones in Japanese gardens into which water trickles. But Murase, who resists being labeled a "Japanese" designer, could probably cite other cultural sources.

Robert Kazuo Murase was born in San Francisco in 1938. As a third-generation Japanese-American, he was taught little about his cultural heritage or language. Nevertheless, he was shipped by train along with his parents, grandparents and other Japanese-Americans to an internment camp designed to protect U.S. national security after Pearl Harbor. At age three, Murase found himself living in tar-papered barracks in Topaz, Utah. Families were crowded into four-by-six rooms and monitored by armed guards. [4] Murase claims little memory of the three-year experience. "It's not that I suffered like my parents and grandparents did," he has said. [5]

After the war, the family returned to live in San Francisco's Japantown. The young Murase pursued interests in design and art—drawing, for example, plans for stage sets for school plays. As a teenager, he was pressed into service to help his uncle, a landscape contractor, build fieldstone garden walls. He says that the experience made no particular impression on him until much later, when he discovered the San Francisco Museum of Modern Art's 1958 Exhibit on Landscape Architecture. "I still have the catalogue," Murase says, which featured models and drawings illustrating the work of the masters of California modernism: Garrett Eckbo, Lawrence Halprin, and Robert Royston. Murase studied landscape architecture at Berkeley, graduating just before the Free Speech Movement exploded on campus. After a two-year Army stint, he worked briefly for both Royston and Halprin. By 1967, Murase had become troubled by his country's involvement in Vietnam, which he viewed as another war against Asian peoples. With little preparation, he moved his young family to Kyoto in order to learn about his cultural background.

Murase spoke no Japanese and had never studied Japan's history, art, or mores. He wrote home that first year, "I find myself a typical *gaijin* (foreigner) here—a stranger within its gates." [6] But he persevered and, through a chance visit to the home of master ceramicist Kawai Kanjiro, began to discover a new cultural and spiritual context for his work. The study of ceramics and of the tea ceremony led him closer to finding his way into Japan's elusive inner nature, providing insights that later informed what is perhaps his most personal, and most powerful work, the Japanese-American Historical Plaza.

While living in Japan, Murase was also greatly influenced by the late Japanese-American sculptor and landscape designer Isamu Noguchi. In the late 1960s Murase was designing a garden for the Japanese Pavilion at Expo '70 in Osaka. Noguchi was in charge of the design of fountains for the entire site. They met while visiting the offices of architect Kenzo Tange to see how their pieces fit into a model of the overall Exposition. As it turned out, the two men shared a passion for collecting Japanese chests, and would later visit antique shops together. On several occasions Murase visited Noguchi's studio on the island of Shikoku, the mother lode for a particularly hard blue granite called "Aji-stone." [7]

Like Noguchi, who was born in Los Angeles and maintained a studio in New York City, Murase became absorbed in his ancestral culture. Noguchi encouraged Murase's study of the gardens of Kyoto and elsewhere in Japan. Murase, already engrossed in his enquiries into Buddhist cosmology, the tea ceremony, the music of the bamboo flute, flower arranging, and folk pottery, explored hundreds of gardens, visiting several repeatedly to study and take photographs. He learned conversational Japanese, meditated, and chanted in temples. But in 1976, having built more projects in Japan than any other American landscape architect, he reluctantly decided to leave. It was largely because of his children. "Japanese children have to attend school for long hours, and there's no time to be a child," he says.

It is also possible that Murase may have found himself compressed between cultures—admittedly uncomfortable with American biases against Asians, but unable to become fully accepted in Japan. When asked if he is a Buddhist, he seems surprised. "Not practicing," he says. "I was baptized Episcopalian." Like his mentor Noguchi, however, he has employed this cultural tension to energize his designs. As Sam Hunter has written of Noguchi, "He has turned the sense of non-belonging, in fact, into a series of courageous and esthetically viable acts of repossession, and managed to combine in triumphant synthesis features of both Eastern and Western tradition." [8]

Portfolio

Japanese-American Historical Plaza

Pier 69 Administrative Headquarters

Nissho Iwai Garden

Collins Circle

Text by Michael Leccese

*Japanese-American
Historical Plaza*

Sure, I go to school

Same as you.

I'm an American.

War and change,
My native land
Once so hard to leave,
Is behind me now
forever.

Going home,
feeling cheated.
Gripping my daughter's hand,
I tell her we're leaving
Without emotion.

GILA

GRENADA

HEART MOUNTAIN

JEROME

MANZANAR

MINIDOKA

POSTON

ROHWER

TOPAZ

TULE LAKE

Pier 69
Port of Seattle
Administrative
Headquarters

Nike Campus
Nissho Iwai Garden

Collins Circle

Japanese-American Historical Plaza

Portland, Oregon

Client: *Oregon Nikkei Endowment*
Date: *1990*

Stone: *Granite from Cascade Mountains*
Amount: *50 tons*
Quarry: *Marenakos*
            Issaquah, Washington

Stone: *Carnelian Granite*
Amount: *100 tons*
Quarry: *Cold Spring, Minnesota*

Stone: *Columbia River Basalt*
Amount: *100 tons*
Quarry: *Interstate Rocks*
            Camus, Washington

The Japanese-American Historical Plaza is a memorial, but unlike many works of landscape architecture of this genre, it is situated in the middle of the city, right on the banks of Portland's Willamette River. From the plaza one can see the city's innermost workings: the historic railroad and highway bridges spanning the Willamette, the shipping piers, the twin spires of the convention center, and the newer office towers of downtown.

One must walk onto the adjacent Burnside Bridge and then look down to view the full design of the plaza. The 1.65-acre site is really much more than a plaza—it is a linear, walk-through history park centered on a circular stone plaza. It includes paths that wind around mounded lawns, and a 275-foot-long, double-curved mound that is faced on its inner surface with paving stones and studded with standing boulders. This long mound, sloping gently on the river side and more sharply on its inner face, is divided in two by the broad, straight central walkway. In plan, these elements combine to form an abstract figure that resembles the spreading wings of a bird, the crane, that in Japan is the symbol for life and happiness. Murase has forcefully manipulated that meaning. Here, the flying crane refers to the "evacuation," as it was called in 1942, of Japanese-American internees—a sorrowful migration that would detain them, away from their homes and normal lives, for the duration of the war.

The memorial adjoins the 1.2-mile-long promenade of Tom McCall Waterfront Park at the edge of the Willamette River, one of the city's most popular places for walking or bicycling. Sinuous pathways intercept cyclists who might disturb those who come to observe or remember. One hundred Japanese cherry trees, donated by the Japanese Wheatgrowers Association, are planted in a double row between the long curved mounds and the straight esplanade which separates the memorial from the river. They form a backdrop, pearly white in spring blossom, crimson in the fall, with the river beyond. The central path enters the site from Front Avenue through a gate formed by massive cylindrical bronze pylons enriched by bas-reliefs. The site is all the more poignant because it is directly across the street from what was once the *Nihonmachi*, or Japantown.

"It is above all a memorable expression of affirmation and forgiveness," architect Joseph Esherick wrote about the plaza. [9] Kenneth I. Helphand, a professor of landscape architecture at the University of Oregon, finds its public aspect just as remarkable. "It's an extraordinary design, with layers of wonderful meaning and symbol," he says. "At the same time, it works for a variety of public uses. People have picnics and play guitars. There's a homeless population. And that doesn't seem discordant. Those uses can co-exist without desecrating the place."

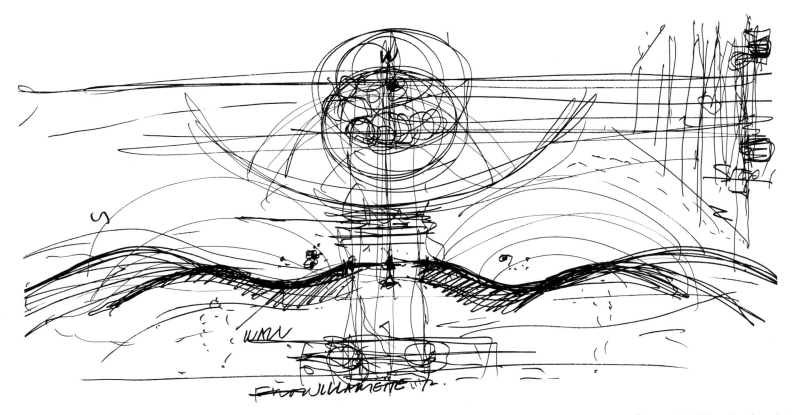

Concept sketch based on feng shui principles

When leading a guest through the plaza on an overcast June day, Murase chooses to start at the south entry along the river. He paces slowly, explaining the unfolding narrative. "This is a series of stories. First it tells the story of people coming to a new land." He sweeps his hand over slabs of basalt set closely, covering the inner face of the long mounds, the spaces between the stones resembling cracks in dry mud. "The wall becomes the community. People gradually building a community. The standing stones emerging from the wall are talking stones. They tell the story. Like the evolving Japanese community, the twelve stones gradually become a wall, solid and whole. Haiku poems describe trying to learn English, starting businesses. Many were written by a woman who was *Issei* (a first-generation immigrant) while in internment. Others were written by an Oregon poet. The poetry makes this memorial so powerful."

Murase comes to a complete stop at the plaza's central circle, composed of broken paving stones. "The wall stops during the war years. History stops. The circle represents the broken lives of families. The center of the plaza also represents mother earth, a place which has the power to restore and nourish the soul. The wall continues and reflects the years following the war, a period of healing and rebuilding."

He pauses beside the monumental bronze pylons on which bas-relief sculpture depicts elements taken from the history of Japanese immigrants in America. One panel represents the 442nd Regimental Combat Team, a U.S. force composed entirely of Japanese-Americans. Children like to trace their fingers on the outlines of the soldiers' faces. He asks, "Did you know this was the most honored unit in the Army?" Not trusted to fight in the Pacific, the 442nd and the 100th Battalion were made up of 21,000 Japanese-American

men who fought with distinction in France and Italy. Nearly 8,000 of them received individual decorations. After the war, both units were honored with a parade down Pennsylvania Avenue and a special citation from President Harry S. Truman. [10]

A plaque at the plaza's entrance reproduces the U.S. Bill of Rights. To explain the connection, Murase refers to a newspaper clipping that describes "the forced exodus" of 110,000 Japanese-Americans; "the only time in U.S. history that the government violated all ten amendments of the Bill of Rights at one time against a single class of citizens." [11] Seventy percent were American-born citizens. In Portland, Oregon, Americans of Japanese ancestry were penned in a stock yard until they could be shipped to ten camps. The experience is remembered in poems carved into one of the plaza's standing boulders, or "talking stones":

Rounded up
in the sweltering yard
Unable to endure any longer
Standing in line, some collapse.

Long before the Japanese-American Historical Plaza was built, Murase dreamed of a memorial to celebrate the history of Japanese immigrants. The late Bill Naito became the idea's benefactor. Naito, a civic-minded Portland developer who helped ignite the city's revival by rehabilitating a series of historic buildings in the 1980s, teamed up with Murase and the sponsoring Oregon Nikkei Foundation in the late 1980s. In his office, Murase keeps the model he used to help raise funds for the idea. His original design called for an amphitheater complete with steps. While Naito worked to persuade the city to include the plaza in the Waterfront Park's master plan, Murase began simplifying his design to meet the needs of an urban site. The steps disappeared, replaced by

One hundred cherry trees

Bronze entry columns

Central plaza

Detail of mother and son
on bronze column

the chest-high mounds, which provide the visibility that police need in order to survey the park.

Meanwhile, Murase selected a simple palette of materials. He chose grey granite pavers in both rectangular and jagged shapes, using fractured slabs of Columbia Gorge basalt to pave the long mounds on their inner faces. For the poetry-inscribed "talking stones," he hand-picked one hundred tons of honey-colored granite from the Snohomish Pass in Washington's Cascade Mountains. His idea for entryway monuments in stone yielded to bronze pylons, a nod to a tradition in public sculpture which at the same time added a layer of texture to his stone compositions. Portland artist Jim Gion made full-size mock-ups of these sculptures in Murase's studio. [12]

Within the composition, the "talking stones" form a kind of sculpture garden of engraved, vertical boulders. One stone carries a list of the names of the ten camps—nothing else. At the center, rectangular pavings embrace a precise circle where the stone resembles pieced-together shards from an eruption. Comments Kenneth Helphand, "That magnificent circle of broken stones re-assembled, which is so beautifully crafted, reminds me of a stained glass window, a rose window."

Helphand's allusion to the creation of whole images from fragments of glass in European cathedrals seems plausible. But Murase's work here more clearly suggests medieval Japanese precedents. Specifically, he has been influenced by the Muromachi period (1333-1573), the era when Zen Buddhism flourished in Japan, and Zen aesthetic principles dictated economy of line and form in a break from more florid earlier styles. In Muromachi garden design, the minimalist concept of *kare sansui* (dry garden)—composed principally of rocks, gravel, and sand, assembled to suggest a dry river bed, rocky islands in the sea, or other natural forms—found expression at many among Kyoto's 2,000 temples. In gardens as in landscape paintings, the outer edge symbolized the vast horizon. "The gardener. . . realised the mountain through the rock, the forest through the moss, and the ocean through the sand," wrote Mark Holborn.[13]

During the civil-war-plagued Shogun era, these meditation gardens were places of mental and physical refuge, where scholars retired to escape not only everyday stresses, but feudal conflict. Notable examples include Ryoan-ji (circa 1488), the walled rectangle of raked quartz and fifteen boulders, and the Abbot's garden at Daisen-in (circa 1339), where 100 stones were carefully placed so as to "poetically evoke an entire world," wrote William Howard Adams.[14] These gardens were built under the supervision of Zen priests in Kyoto, Japan's capital for a millennium. Added Adams, "These austere spaces excelled in enhancing the inner life of the faithful, which further helped them in the selection and placing of garden stones."[15]

Whether Murase was influenced by Ryoan-ji or any particular Muromachi garden is difficult to ascertain. Perhaps mindful of the era's creative imperatives, he sometimes hesitates to discuss sources in detail. "As soon as the striving for beauty was self-conscious, forced or pretentious," wrote Holborn, "then beauty was lost. Beauty flourished where there was the least desire to create it—in the accidents of nature. The tea masters of the Muromachi period fully understood this principle and further developed it in their appreciation of the simple, uncontrived quality of the rough folk-wares of rural craftsmen. The role of the artist was to act as an agent through which beauty took form, not as a creator or controller extracting beauty."[16]

Elevation through the center of the plaza

Stone assembly

"Ten camps"

Philosophically, Murase was also influenced by the idea of *wabi*, an aesthetic concept that values solitude and sees beauty in simplicity. One expression of these qualities is the elaborately scripted tea ceremony. Wrote Murase, "This emptiness is active and draws its strength from the soil of its own nature, life experience, and tradition, and has a bright spirit which communicates freely and directly. *Wabi*, an essential element in the art of flower arrangement for the tea ceremony, is a state of emptiness, coldness, poverty, and solitude. These attributes seem negative and uncreative. However, in *wabi* there is a rich spirit." [17]

Murase developed his physical craft in the designing and building of several projects in Japan. One, *Myodo Kyo Kai*, a new Buddhist temple complex in Shiga Prefecture, won an Honor Award from the American Society of Landscape Architects in 1980. [18] For six weeks Murase worked there with two masons, placing each stone with ten-ton cranes.

He described this process as an emotional and religious extension of Shinto. In short, the masons weren't placing stones merely for aesthetic or even functional reasons; they were revealing the spirit of these sacred stones (*Iwakura*), each imbued with its own soul. As Mark Holborn wrote: "Religious veneration is still an active part of the Japanese experience of nature. Through Shinto, 'the way of the gods,' the natural elements have been endowed with holy properties known as 'Kami.' . . . Forms which Westerners would consider inanimate have become fused with a vitality through Shinto. Whereas we in the West would mould or break natural form to our own design, the Japanese, recognizing the vitality inherent in the form, shape the design to release the vitality." [19]

"I am filled with admiration for what you have accomplished," Noguchi wrote to Murase regarding *Myodo Kyo Kai*. [20] But Noguchi also warned the

landscape architect against trying to replicate such Japanese stonecraft in America. For this reason, Murase invited the sculptor's own mason from Shikoku to consult for two weeks on construction of the Japanese-American Historical Plaza. Masatoshi Izumi is a fourth-generation mason whose family has been working with stone for 250 years. Murase was particularly concerned about making the basalt corners come together at the break in the wall. Izumi, who speaks no English, directed crews through gestures and by using a hand tool to make faint white marks indicating where stone should be cut. [21]

Murase described the nature of his collaboration with Japanese stone masons: "As I selected a stone for its place and indicated its top and front, the masons would tie it with steel cables and direct the crane operator to the selected area. As this was being done, I would choose the next stone, and have a good feeling for the size and shape of the fol-

lowing stone. Placing the stone was critical, for it had to be exact. An eighth of an inch in the wrong direction would be enormously wrong. . . .

"[W]e began to work intuitively together. Because of this integral relationship, work would virtually come to a standstill if I had to go to a meeting . . . Likewise, if one of the masons couldn't come to work . . . work on the walls would stop." [22]

Elevation from the Front Street entrance

0   20 feet

"Talking Stones"

"Going Home"

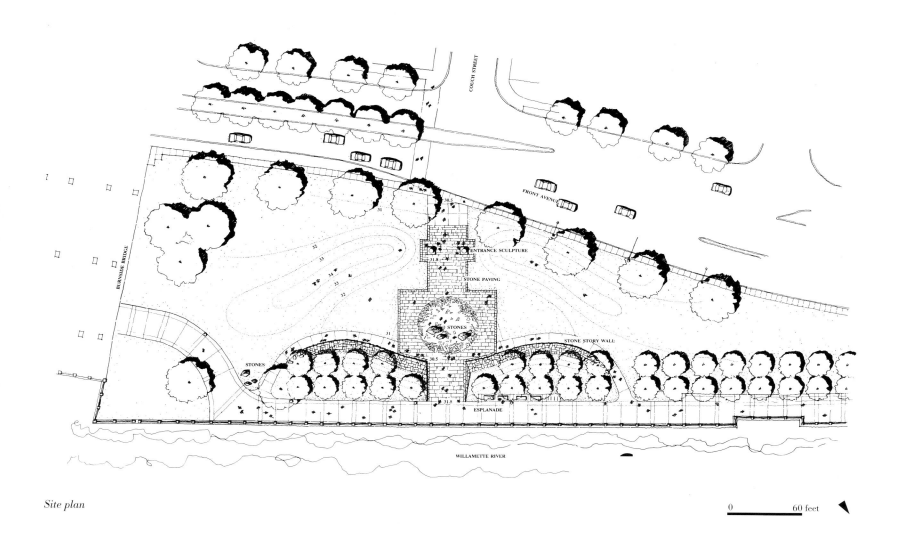

Site plan

0 ——————— 60 feet

Project under construction

Fractured granite circle

Setting the poetry stone

Mock-up of poetry for engraving

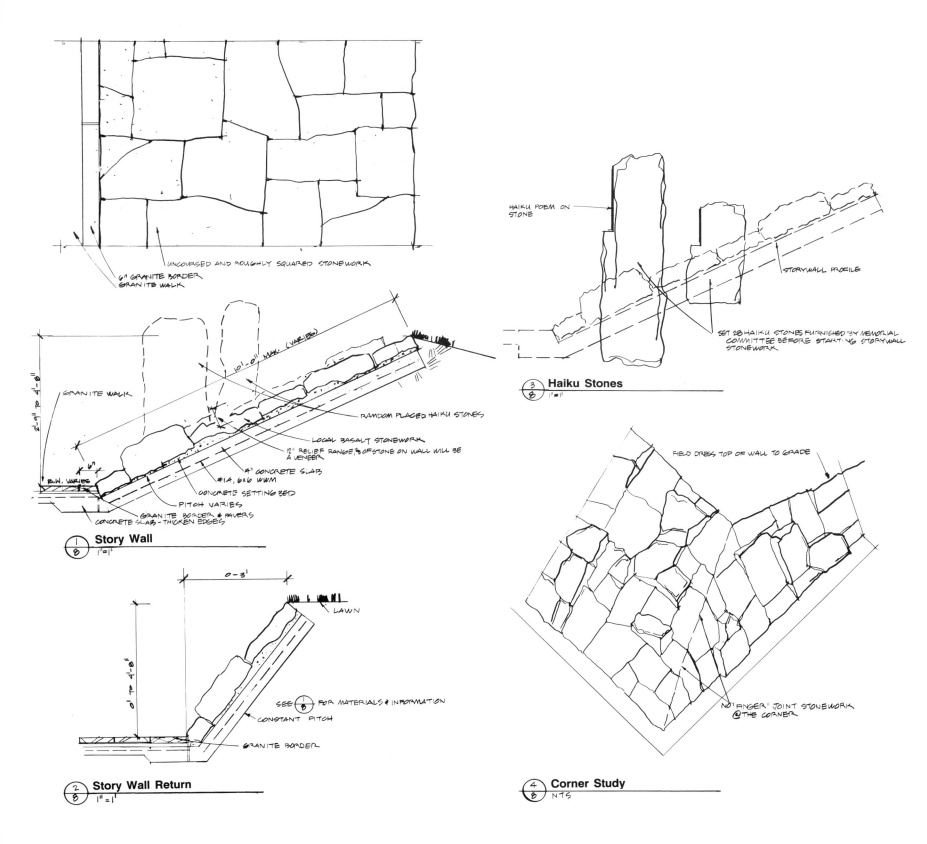

UNCOURSED AND ROUGHLY SQUARED STONEWORK

6" GRANITE BORDER
GRANITE WALK

HAIKU POEM ON STONE

STORYWALL PROFILE

SET 28 HAIKU STONES FURNISHED BY MEMORIAL COMMITTEE BEFORE STARTING STORYWALL STONEWORK

③/⑧ Haiku Stones 1"=1'

GRANITE WALK

10'-0" MAX. (VARIES)

2'-9" TO 4'-8"

B.W. VARIES

6"

RANDOM PLACED HAIKU STONES

LOCAL BASALT STONEWORK

12" RELIEF RANGE - STONE ON WALL WILL BE A VENEER

4" CONCRETE SLAB

#1A, 6x6 WWM

CONCRETE SETTING BED

PITCH VARIES

GRANITE BORDER & PAVERS

CONCRETE SLAB - THICKEN EDGES

①/⑧ Story Wall 1"=1'

0-3'

0' TO 4'-8"

LAWN

SEE ⑧ FOR MATERIALS & INFORMATION

CONSTANT PITCH

GRANITE BORDER

②/⑧ Story Wall Return 1"=1'

FIELD DRESS TOP OF WALL TO GRADE

NO "FINGER" JOINT STONEWORK @ THE CORNER

④/⑧ Corner Study NTS

Stone construction details

Pier 69 Port of Seattle Administrative Headquarters
Seattle, Washington

Client: Port of Seattle
Date: 1994

Stone: *Lake Placid Blue Granite*
Quarry: *Cold Spring Granite Company
           Cold Spring, Minnesota*

Stone: *Burlington Slate*
Quarry: *Burlington Natstone
           Plano, Texas*

When discussing his current work, Murase often refers to his interest in pottery. What does he expect to see and hear when he turns on a fountain or runnel for the first time? "It's just like a ceramic piece you put into a kiln for a week and you see what happens—lots of surprises. Usually good surprises." Water may braid or run in smooth sheets. It will generally whisper. Visiting Islamic gardens in southern Spain, Murase learned to be spare with water. "I took out my tape measure and I was surprised at how little water depth you need to really feel the quality," he says. "They weren't very wide or deep at all. The first one *I* did was made out of concrete, and a foot deep."

Murase's work with water and stone at Seattle's Pier 69 Atrium is more subtle than that earlier effort. This precisely machined, almost spartan indoor garden, where the designer applied Islamic as well as Japanese and Modernist design principles, consists of only two types of stone—and no plants. Situated in a waterfront building converted from a salmon can-

nery, the Atrium measures more than 700 feet long. It is bisected by a runnel that flows for four hundred feet, but is only one inch deep. Yet the murmur of the water effectively masks sounds both of the city and from within cavernous, open-plan offices.

Visitors arrive at street level and proceed up a cantilevered staircase that seems to float through the space. This leads to a large, long room defined by massive, exposed concrete columns, balconies, and the office cubicles of Port employees. The fountain begins at the far end of the space, flowing out of a tall, obelisk-like piece of curved, smooth stone into the runnel, a central channel that flows between eight shorter pedestal-seats. Arranged symmetrically, these granite pedestals contain notches from which more sheets of water spill into the runnel, which then curves along a half-ellipse created by a long stone bench. After strolling along this stream, visitors walk through an elevator lobby into a smaller room. The eye is again directed to the farthest end of the space, where water bubbles out from an angled

cube of stone into another, shorter runnel. A slightly curved stair, with slate treads and ship-like railings, projects to the left, and leads to a view of Elliott Bay and the distant Olympic Range.

Light patterns from skylights complete the composition. Even on frequent overcast days, this light is strengthened by the reflection of sky off water on three sides of the pier. The composition includes nothing soft, green or "gardenesque." "I thought it would be unfortunate if some plant leasing company were allowed to decorate this space," says Murase. "So I had to have a commitment that they wouldn't clutter it up with tropical plants."

Made from polished granite that reflects a cold bluish light, the fountains and runnels are set into a floor of meticulously laid slate pavers. The feeling is of an ideal street, clean, quiet, and uncluttered. Indeed, the Atrium functions wonderfully well as public space. "We've had political rallies, group tours, office meetings, even weddings," says David Hewitt, the chief architect for the building renovation, who praises the flexibility of Murase's plan.

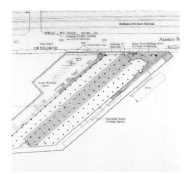

Site plan

Granite tower

Central atrium axis

Curved entry bench and runnel

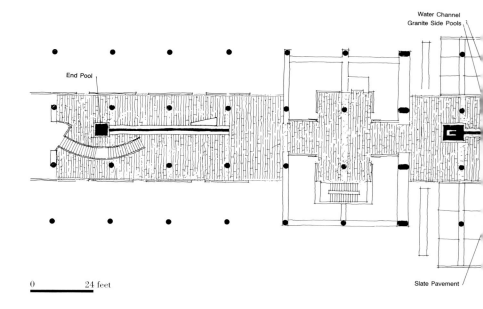

Atrium plan

"The space is a conduit for people and conversation."

"This *is* an urban street," insists Port Commissioner Paul Schell. "Murase has created a sense of dignity and drama that's urban. It's not an overdone suburban atrium. In part, it's just a practical way to deal with noise. But it also represents this region and the Port with very subtle, Zen-like symbols. This works for us in the sense that most of our marine customers are Asians."

When Murase joined the Port project as a consultant, he had never worked on an interior space. In 1991, the Port of Seattle assembled a large team of designers to renovate the 1931 American Can Company building. Since American Can abandoned the building twenty years ago, it had become a "pigeon roost," recalls Schell. Located on Seattle's industrial/tourist waterfront on Pier 69, the two-story, reinforced-concrete building juts into Elliott Bay at a forty-one degree angle from Alaskan Way. [23] The team leaders, Seattle architects Hewitt Isley, planned to cut a 750-foot-long atrium into the top

two floors of the 210,000-square-foot building. (They couldn't use the bottom floor, as it is reserved as the passenger lobby for a ferry that docks at Pier 69.) The new space would provide both a focal point and gathering place for the Port's 325 employees. Hewitt reasoned that since the building has almost no exterior space for a plaza or gardens, why not make the Atrium an "interior landscape"? Hewitt had admired Murase's use of materials at the Japanese-American Historical Plaza and asked him to join the team.

The landscape architect's preliminary idea was a gardenesque attempt to express the Port's purpose symbolically through oceanic imagery. In his office in Portland, Murase fetches his "rough draft," a clay model about three feet long. At first, he envisioned a garden consisting of curved, planted mounds of earth flanked by crescent-shaped pools. The scheme suggested "waves in the ocean with eddies and pools"—and it pleased the clients.

As so often happens with Murase, most of these ideas were jettisoned on his way toward the final scheme. The Atrium

was eventually constituted only of water, slate, and flecked granite that is either polished or flame-finished. A cool, slate-blue dominates the palette so thoroughly that the space photographs just as well in black-and-white as in color. (Five large skylights angled into the sawtooth roof admit the consistently bright, yet diffused light.) The mounds of the first scheme were replaced by the polished, angular granite pedestals that both flank the runnel and feed sheets of water into it. A low granite bench and floating stone stairs survive as curved elements from the earlier scheme. His clients accepted this change of direction. "Some people asked where the garden went," says Murase, "but they liked the plan."

To fully grasp the implications of space and materials at this magnitude, Murase wanted to work at full scale. So he made full-sized cardboard models of individual features. With his associates, he then chalked out the site plan onto the streets outside his studio. Next he developed precise architectural drawings, another departure, as Murase's drawings

generally serve only as guides to how much stone to purchase. He also addressed the issue of weight. Since the atrium is located on the second floor, he could not use solid stone; its heft would exceed both floor-depth standards and the load-bearing capacity of the building, even though the thirty-inch columns were built to withstand immense sheet rolls for cans. So Murase employed stone veneer. The seams are clearly visible where modular stone panels are joined. Yet the treatment of the corners—of the fountainheads, for instance, which are angled like a ship's prow—makes each pedestal or bench seem solid as a boulder when, in fact, they are all hollow.

The Pier 69 Atrium also incorporates eight commissioned works by Northwest public artists. The most notable (and noticeable) piece is Nancy Hammer's brushed-aluminum transformation of two interior columns into underwater piers, replete with barnacles, mussels, and seaweed. Yet the literalness of several of these artworks only seems to emphasize the strength of Murase's abstract composition.

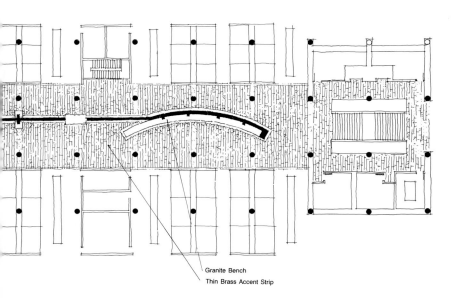

Granite Bench
Thin Brass Accent Strip

Granite cube

Bridge view of granite tower

Reflection of water

View from above

In comparison, some of the public artists' explorations seem like mere decoration. Murase's Atrium contains an inherent richness that allows it (like the Japanese-American Plaza) to function in varied ways while remaining open to many interpretations. It could remind one person of an Islamic courtyard, another of a Zen garden.

At the same time, by providing equal access to light and air for all employees, the Atrium is consistent with the Port's egalitarian structure, where all offices, even for commissioners, measure twelve-by-twelve. Many cubicles open directly onto the Atrium. Acoustic panels prevent excessive noise from disturbing employees, although their visual access allows them to feel included in all Port events and activities. Moreover, the Atrium revives the idea of the grand interior-corridor-as-courtyard. In early skyscrapers, this amenity reached high expression in such Chicago buildings as the Monadnock addition of 1893 and the Old Colony Building of 1894, [24] themselves inspired

by Milan's Galleria Vittorio Emanuele II, a huge glass-roofed shopping arcade completed in 1878. "When most people come up the stairs and see the space, they just gasp, because it is so restful," says Hewitt. "But this is really a place about work. The clarity of the plan expresses an intensity about the goings-on, a purposefulness in the air."

Oregonian critic Randy Gragg is reminded of architect Louis I. Kahn's outdoor courtyard for the Salk Institute in La Jolla, California. "It's hard not to think of Kahn," he says. "Both places feature a linear water element heading out to the sound, but Pier 69 has a totally different feel. It yields in a way that Kahn's doesn't. The Port project is an invitation. It draws you near. In La Jolla you have a powerful spatial composition with an ancient, almost archetypal power to it. With the Port of Seattle, you have all those elements, yet it is a soothing gesture rather than a powerful gesture."

Construction of atrium

Construction of pedestal seat

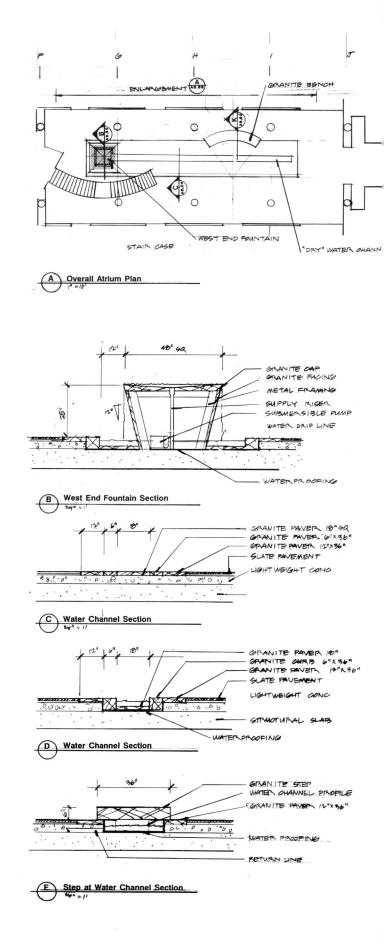

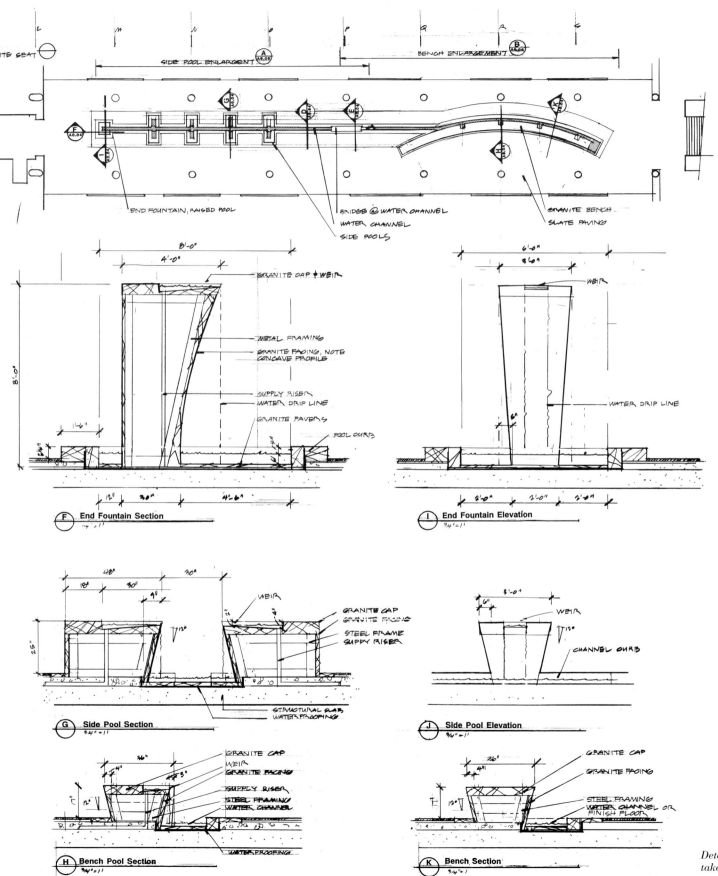

Detailed construction plan and sections
taken from contract drawings

Nike Campus Nissho Iwai Garden
Portland, Oregon

Client: *Nike, Inc.*
Date: *1992*

Stone: *Heather Stone*
Amount: *75 tons*
Quarry: *Interstate Rocks Quarry*
         White Pass, Washington

The Japanese film maker Akira Kurosawa is another influence Murase likes to cite. The landscape architect conceives of space cinematically, always highly conscious of how people will regard places when moving by in cars, trains, or on foot. "Motion is so important," he says. This concern for movement is evident at his Nissho Iwai Garden at Nike World Headquarters in Beaverton, Oregon. The $65 million, 174-acre corporate campus is circumscribed by a wood-chip jogging path, and includes a formal lake, outdoor cafeteria plaza, preserved wetlands, flags and banners, as well as realistic sculptures of reclining figures by J. Seward Johnson. Nike employs 2,500 people, and many of them use the company product. So each day hundreds of joggers run by the Nissho Iwai Garden. Yet it is as intimate, picturesque and meditative as the rest of Nike's campus landscape architecture is expansive and frenetic.

The Nissho Iwai garden expresses the spontaneity of a natural area although it is indeed fabricated. Next to a lushly planted mound, a stream bed intersects with a mill-race lined by rough-stacked stone. On an early summer day, purple irises pack the edges of the stream, which can be crossed on stepping stones. A hummingbird hovers at an iris bloom; a goldfinch hangs upon a willow. Boulders seem to tumble out of the creek into the shallow edge of the lake. The slender, almost spidery boughs of Japanese maples reflect in the still waters of the mill channel. One of Murase's goals here was to detain the joggers for at least a moment, so he offered them an "alternate path," threaded through a mound planted with Japanese maple, cherry trees, rhododendron, and red-twig dogwood. "I wanted to incorporate a place of pause," he says.

In 1974, Nike founder Phil Knight was attempting to raise money for his fledgling sneaker venture. Shunned by American investors, he was rescued by a cash infusion from a Japanese trading company called Nissho Iwai. In 1992, as his company neared its twentieth anniversary, Knight wanted to honor Nissho Iwai with a garden party. The problem was that although his campus (designed largely by OTAK of Lake Oswego, Oregon), seemed to offer every conceivable landscape feature, there was no intimate garden setting in which the party could be given. [25] Knight asked Murase to make a "Japanese" garden near the metal-clad Building H—also known as the Nolan Ryan Building. "I kept saying, what *is* a Japanese garden?" recalls Murase.

Given such scant programmatic direction, Murase decided to relate the lake to adjacent wetlands. The connection he devised is a natural-looking streamlet that trickles over smooth river stones and around blocky boulders to merge with the

Stream channel

Stone and gravel path

Setting the stone

Water source

Water over stone

"Level the stone"

marsh. Next to this delicate water feature, he built a mounded garden using earth excavated from other construction sites on the campus. The garden needed an "edge," and Murase created another water feature with the character of a mill sluiceway. This narrow, stone-lined channel runs perpendicular to the stream. Along its course, less than an inch of water sheets over a cobbled bed and tips over two weir-like structures. The channel's low walls are made from stacked andesite, a hard, white-grey stone cut oblong like Roman bricks. They contain the flow, which bends hard around two right-angled walls. The viewer might be reminded of a tiny canal drawing from, and then merging with, a seasonal stream. In fact, the stream is dry unless the lake overflows, while the stone chute is continuously fed by a recirculating pump submerged in the lake.

Murase's inspirations were not limited to Japanese precedents. "The stream design abstracts various design forms from the Islamic tradition, the Japanese tradition, English romantic gardens, and nature too," he says. "It's a collage of images, but it's nothing stylized. There are basic design elements that can be interpreted to evoke different images, real, primordial, symbolic, but down-to-earth with a sense of mystery that lets the participant finish the picture. That's an important feature of Japanese art."

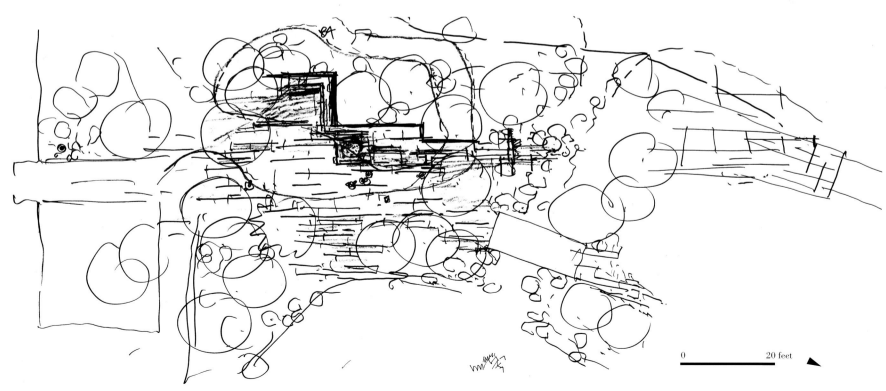

Concept sketch

Collins Circle

Portland, Oregon

Client: *Tri-Met*
Date: *1996*

Stone: *Windswept Basalt*
Amount: *485 tons*
Quarry: *Interstate Rocks Quarry*
Camas, Washington

On the western perimeter of downtown Portland, Oregon, the Goose Hollow neighborhood has long retained its small-town character, with big trees and wood-frame houses. The neighborhood's geographic center is a traffic circle called Collins Circle. Before the 1960s, Collins Circle was an eyesore, a forest of utility poles where several utility lines merged. Then a local foundation, inspired by Lady Bird Johnson's national beautification campaign, paid to have the circle converted into a simple park with grass, mounds, and trees.

Today Collins Circle is the epicenter of a changing neighborhood. Right next to the circle, large new luxury apartment buildings signify imminent big-city congestion as well as impending gentrification. Just beyond these structures, a new transit station is being built as part of Portland's 15-mile, billion-dollar light-rail extension. A visitor getting reacquainted with the neighborhood in 1996 might walk past Portland's minor-league baseball stadium to find torn-up streets being reassembled, the trolley tracks set into grey cobble pavers.

Then, that visitor might be shocked to find that Collins Circle has been stripped of its park. In its place is a tilted eight-foot high assemblage of grey boulders. Although these boulders appear to be rough-laid (they are actually mortared together deep in the cracks between stones), they form a perfect portion of a circle, about one-hundred feet in diameter. In plan, the circle resembles two overlapping half-moons. Its edges form a smooth, angled wall. The top is a curved shallow depression studded with upright boulders and a few small trees. *Oregonian* critic Gragg calls the piece "one of the boldest pieces of public art since (Lawrence Halprin's) Lovejoy Fountain."

Its purpose may seem mysterious. But the revamped Collins Circle addresses a straightforward safety concern. It is designed to discourage people from crossing traffic lanes and train tracks to get to it: the new circle is not particularly hospitable for walking, picnicking, or sleeping. This daringly simple solution belongs to Murase, who served as the landscape architect for the initial 12-mile portion of Portland's light-rail system, as well as for the 6-mile extension.

The landscape architect was inspired by the basic shape of the traffic circle, which reminded him of stone circles and "other historical megalithic places. . . . The tradition of stone circles is such a powerful one. They are symbols of gods, places of burial, places that filled the hearts of people, places of protection, of mother earth, of guardian spirits." During the development of models and drawings, he initially conceived a stone circle containing a fountain or waterfall. As he edited, the circle lost its water feature. Plantings were removed or simplified. The plane of the circle became tilted and concave and a large piece was sliced out of the side facing the tracks. "The circle was very obvious," he says. "How we interpreted the circle was much more complex."

View from station platform

The slice in the circle

Stone outcroppings

Growing out of the cracks

Collins Circle is one of the first things transit riders will see after their trains emerge from a nearby tunnel. So Murase calls his concept a "gateway" or "a marker at the city's edge." He also sought to project an image from regional ecology: lava flows in central Oregon, where piles of rock are dotted with sprouting vegetation. At Collins Circle, a few gnarled sumacs growing from cracks between the rocks create a similar image. Stone circle, geologic formation—Murase had one more last-minute improvisation in mind. It involved addition rather than subtraction, for a change. He decided to place a half-dozen standing boulders on the surface of the plane. "We thought it would be interesting to make something pointed toward the sky that would add to the tension of the circle. It required getting more boulders and going through the public (review) process again." Given neighborhood grumbling related to the loss of the park-like space at Collins Circle, this was a courageous move, but Murase prevailed.

One more source inspired him: Enso, a symbol from Japanese Zen Buddhism. The Enso interprets the circle as a void encompassed by an unending line that represents the artist's enlightenment. [26] Characteristically, Murase will mention these symbolic sources only when pressed, and he denies that they acquire any particular new meaning in their urban setting. Instead, he focuses on how this piece meets the client's needs. He was asked to design a set-piece to ward off encampments of transients (the tilted, rough stones are almost impossible to walk on)—one that train-riders would enjoy viewing from their seats. "Although Collins Circle is not loaded with meaning," says Murase, "it gives people something to think about. It creates a landscape that is a spiritual place, although we only pass it momentarily."

Field of basalt

View from Vista Bridge

Detail of stonework

Angling the edge

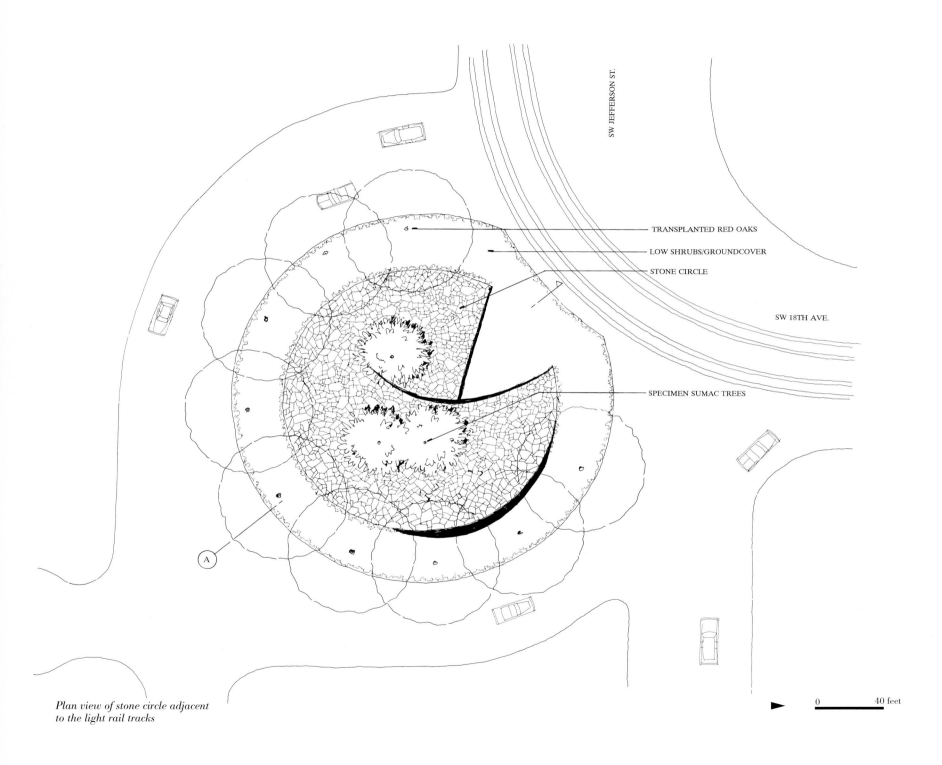

SW JEFFERSON ST.

TRANSPLANTED RED OAKS

LOW SHRUBS/GROUNDCOVER

STONE CIRCLE

SW 18TH AVE.

SPECIMEN SUMAC TREES

A

*Plan view of stone circle adjacent
to the light rail tracks*

0   40 feet

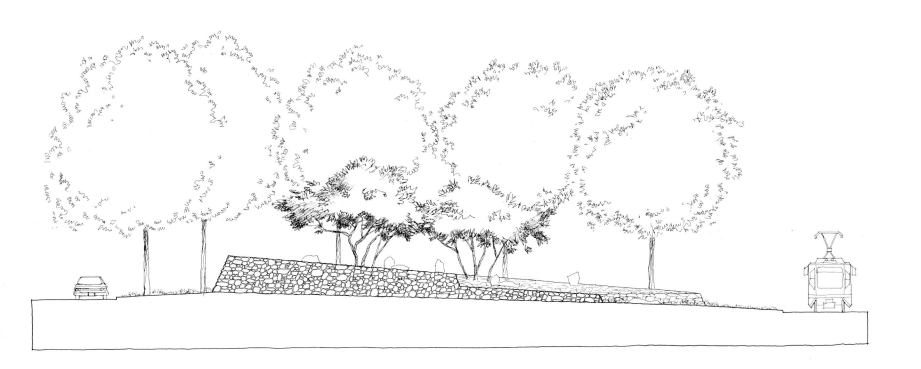

Elevation of stone circle

0 ⎯⎯⎯⎯ 16 feet

Portfolio

NEC America Campus, Inc.

Corporate Headquarters

Green Center

Myodo Kyo Kai

Private Residence

Project descriptions by
Murase Associates

NEC America Campus, Inc.

Green Center

Myodo Kyo Kai

Private Residence

NEC America Campus
Hillsboro, Oregon

Client: *NEC America, Inc.*
Date: *1986*

Stone: *Recycled sandstone from old building foundations and lintels*

Amount: *140 tons*

At NEC America's 200-acre corporate park in Hillsboro, Oregon, Murase designed the campus landscape plan and markedly, varied, interior courtyards. An employee entry leads to a courtyard paved with smooth rectangular tiles, around which the corporate offices, conference rooms, lobby, and cafeteria are situated. A water cascade feeds a long pool of sandstone blocks that occupies one side of the linear space. Murase paid as much attention to the abstract composition of the underwater rocks as to those on the surface. Traditional plantings of Japanese maples, rhododendrons, azaleas, and spireas play against the geometry of the water feature, and impart a lyricism to the design theme.

By contrast, the second courtyard, composed only of gravel, stone, and bamboo, is symmetrical, spare, yet very elegant. A block of closely planted bamboo, with slender stalks and delicate yellow foliage, stands at one end of the inner courtyard. At the other is a stone water basin, its sides rough-cut from a single sandstone block.

The courtyards constitute dramatically complementary spaces, which function both as outdoor places under the sky, and as part of the experience of the buildings' interiors.

Terrace view from cafeteria

Water cascade

Movement of water over stone

Stone and water detail

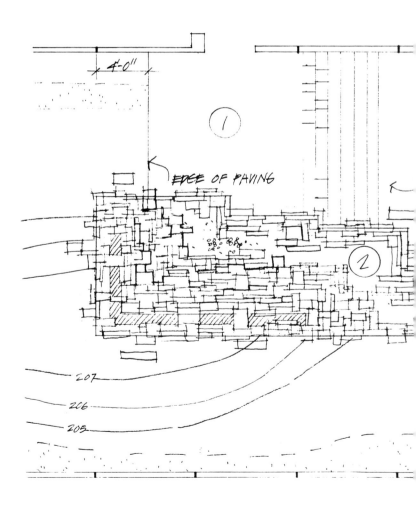
Stone arrangement diagram

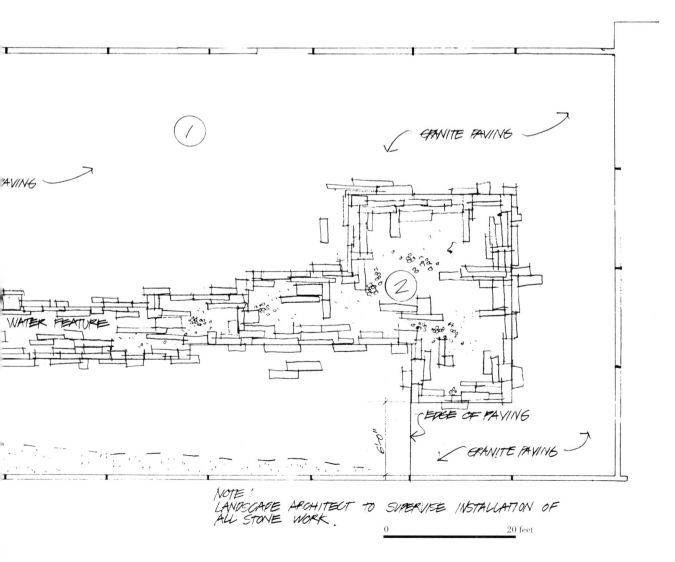

①

PAVING

GRANITE PAVING

WATER FEATURE

②

EDGE OF PAVING

6'-0"

GRANITE PAVING

NOTE:
LANDSCAPE ARCHITECT TO SUPERVISE INSTALLATION OF
ALL STONE WORK.

0   20 feet

View from conference room

View from sitting area

Corporate Headquarters
Redmond, Washington

Date: 1996

Stone: *Carnelian Granite*
Amount: *108 tons*
Quarry: *Cold Spring Granite Company*
          Cold Spring, Minnesota

Stone: *Windswept Basalt*
Amount: *1780 tons*
Quarry: *Interstate Rocks*
          Camas, Washington

Stone: *Columnar Basalt*
Amount: *180 tons*
Quarry: *Interstate Rocks*
          Eastern Washington

In this project Murase employs a characteristic positioning of work precisely at the point where the work of man and nature meet. He uses elements which are obviously manufactured, cut and shaped into simple geometric forms—and natural forms—flowing water, uncut stone. He manages to juxtapose and combine the two idioms to coexist in a state of harmonious tension.

The sloping topography of the corporate office headquarters was significant in designing the landscape for the site. Murase wove the various buildings together with a series of walls, plazas, terraces, and water features.

The activity of the water varies from place to place, at times confined to a narrow channel, at others broadening into a still reflecting pool or rushing over rocks in a series of waterfalls. The most dramatic falls, built from a layered composition of columnar basalt, are situated near the lower terrace.

Columnar basalt waterfall

Pools adjacent to the cafeteria terrace

Water cascade

"Mother Stone"

Sketch plan for the water course

290

0   40 feet ▲

Constructing the cascade and pool

Setting the "Mother Stone"

Constructing the cafeteria entrance waterfalls

Constructing the cascade

Green Center

Aichi Prefecture, Japan

Date: 1974
Client: *Aichi Prefecture*

Stone: *Local Granite*

Green Center is a botanical garden and conference center developed for Aichi Prefecture in Japan. The broadly spaced entrance plaza is a transition landscape that connects a conference center with a Japanese garden, a botanical garden, and a parking area. An arriving visitor walks up broad steps, set between trees, to the edge of the plaza. A wide plain of precisely set, rectangular granite pavers, the plaza gently slopes down to a pool. Radiating at intervals from the pool are long, shallow channels. Emerging from the pool as if erupted from the organized pattern of the cut stone paving are irregular blocks of granite, masterfully fitted together. Though it is apparent that they are man-made, they are entirely convincing as natural forms. The geometric paving of the plaza shimmers beneath the clear water of the pool.

The plaza is imbued with the sense of a deeply reassuring, harmonious co-existence between the works of man and nature. The generous scale of the interrelated spaces, and the consistency of the meticulous craftsmanship throughout, combine to give the space a quality of ceremonial significance. The main plaza is more than one hundred feet across, and connects by broad steps to other paved open spaces edged by large trees. A combination of rock-strewn plain and welcoming civic space, the plaza is big enough to accommodate Japanese tourists who normally travel in large groups, but when empty, is stunningly effective—remarkable and moving.

Pavers sloping down to pool

Fractured granite formations

Construction of stonework

Stone eruption

Angular stone formation

Shards of granite

54

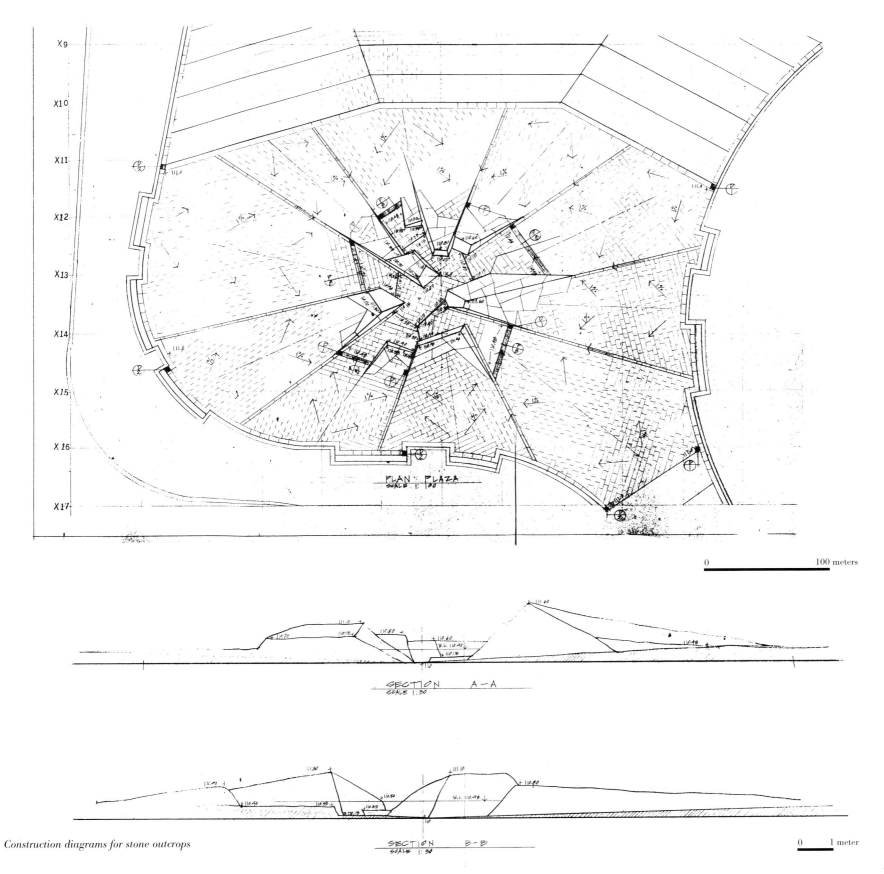

PLAN · PLAZA
SCALE 1: 30

0   100 meters

Construction diagrams for stone outcrops

SECTION   A—A
SCALE 1: 30

SECTION   B—B
SCALE 1: 30

0   1 meter

Myodo Kyo Kai

Shiga Prefecture, Japan

Client: *Myodo Kyo Kai*
Date: *1975*

Stone: *Local Granite*

Myodo Kyo Kai is a Buddhist temple complex in the rural Shiga Prefecture of Japan. Perched atop a long hill in the foothills of the mountain range that separates Kyoto and Shiga Prefecture, the site was once a series of terraced rice fields. The entrance to the temple complex is at the southern end of the site, and takes the form of a long and broad ceremonial pathway which leads between two rows of evenly spaced deciduous trees. The pathway is constructed of rectangular blocks of granite set between wide bands of packed crushed stone out of which the trees grow. At the end of this pathway there is a broad plaza, the Prayer Square, where a line of bamboo dippers is set out by the purification pool for worshippers to use in cleansing their hands. Some may choose to receive the water in cupped hands as it flows over the edge of the pool. On the east side of the Prayer Square, behind a low wall, a shallow water course flows among blocky granite boulders. Pilgrimage to the temple complex traditionally follows a series of religious events that culminate at the upper open space which faces a tower and a 21-foot waterfall.

This project received an American Society of Landscape Architects Honor Award. Excerpted jury comments include, "Only a true artist can create something of this nature and quality. . . . It is very beautiful and recaptures the spiritual values in the making of the environment. . . ."

Ceremonial walkway

Prayer square

Entry wall construction

Detail of water cascade

*Purification pool
and bamboo dippers*

Water cascade

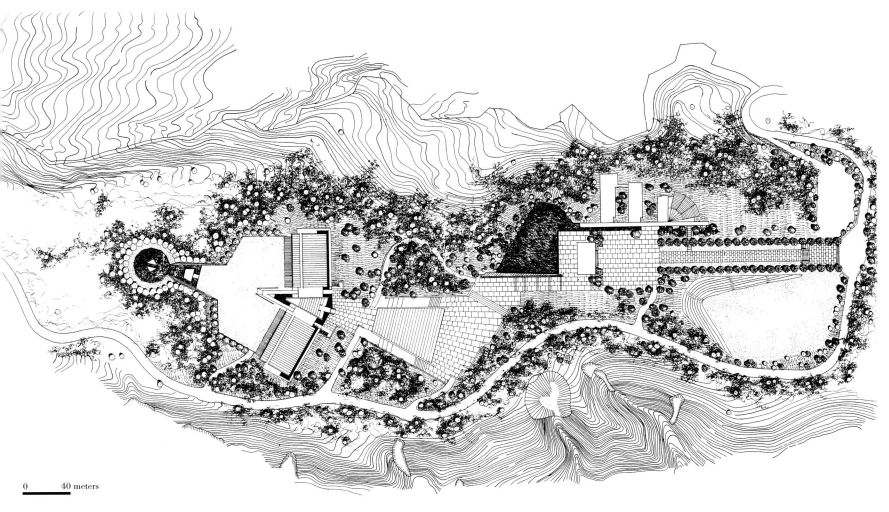

0   40 meters

Site plan

Private Residence

Bloomfield Hills, Michigan

Date: 1990

Stone: *Local Sandscone*
Amount: *20 tons*

This narrow garden, built for a private residence, is a classic example of a "viewing garden," and is evocative of a small Japanese interior courtyard. It is designed for the pleasure and refreshment of people looking out from the house, which is glass-walled where it faces the garden. The client lived in Japan for many years, and was well aware of how such small courtyard gardens, connected visually to a room or rooms, could transform a house and allow new dimensions of landscape scale and understanding.

The horizontal lines of the prairie are recalled in the rocks of a honey-colored sandstone waterfall, where the water drops into a pool dotted with stepping stones. The wall here is curved, and set with small horizontal pieces of a local sandstone, which Robert Murase discovered in the course of a field trip. He remembers, "We used a group of brick-layers to lay up the stone, and, of course I had to get them to loosen up. 'Place the stone like Mohammed Ali would move,' I said. Placing stone, like design, is always intuitive, and how water will move over stone is something I always look forward to with anticipation." The horizontal lines of the sandstone are interrupted by a large, roughly triangular, flat stone set vertically, the whole constituting an abstract design.

Water source

Rhythmic layering of sandstone

Stone detail

Construction of curving sandstone waterfall

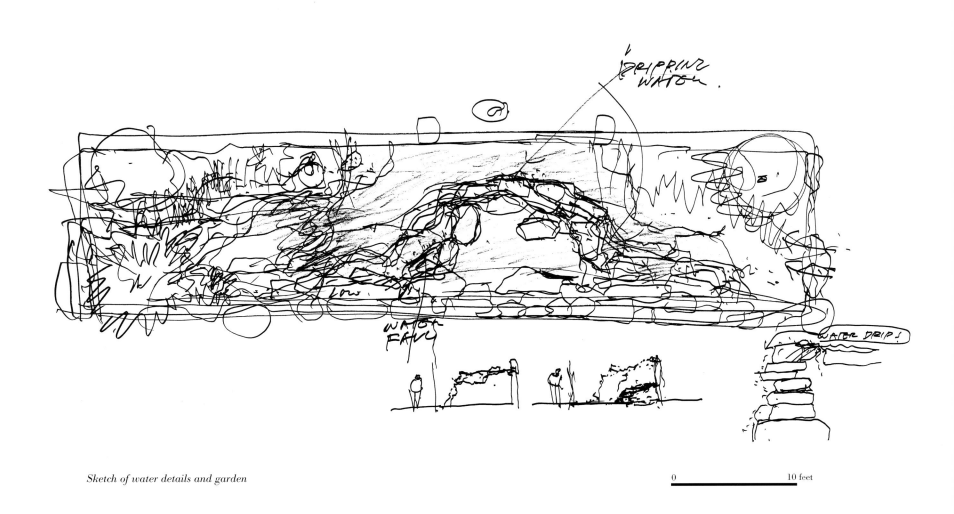

Sketch of water details and garden

Robert K. Murase

Robert Murase is a landscape architect with thirty years of experience, whose work can be found in the United States, Japan, the Pacific Basin and the Caribbean. His projects have been featured in architectural magazines, journals, and books.

After graduating from the University of California at Berkeley with a BLA in Landscape Architecture, Mr. Murase apprenticed at the offices of Robert Royston and Lawrence Halprin. To further enrich his experience, he moved to Japan, where he practiced for nearly ten years, initially doing garden research at Kyoto University. Subsequently, he taught at the University of Oregon's Department of Landscape Architecture, after which he worked for EDAW in Portland, Oregon. In 1982, he established his own studio in Portland, opening a Seattle office in 1988.

Mr. Murase has designed courtyards and unique spaces for museums, libraries, hospitals, schools, and municipal buildings. He has been responsible for the master planning and design for visitor and resort complexes, university campuses, and park and recreation developments. His projects include a major port redevelopment, housing and new town facilities, and regional development for the preservation of historic temple ruins. Planning projects in Indonesia include the regional development plan for tourism in Yogyakarta; the Borobudur Archaeological Center and Prambanan Temple landscape plan; and the Pasia Angin Resort.

Urban design projects include the Port of Seattle Central Waterfront Design Guidelines, the Astoria Waterfront Plan and the Wilsonville Town Center Park in Oregon, and the Goshogawara Civic Core District Development Plan in Japan. He was responsible for the site plan of the University of Washington's Physics, Chemistry, and Electrical Engineering Buildings, which comprise much of the historical central campus. Other projects include a 36-acre high-tech corporate campus in Redmond, Washington, and the Benaroya Concert Hall Garden of Remembrance in downtown Seattle.

Robert Murase has been a guest lecturer and speaker at universities, museums, arboretums, and other institutions. A frequent participant in symposiums and seminars, he has also served on design juries in the United States and Japan. He is a fellow of the American Society of Landscape Architects. A book tracing one hundred years of Japanese American history, *Touching the Stones*, is based on Mr. Murase's design of the Japanese American Historical Plaza.

Photo Credits

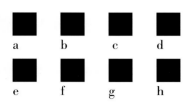

a   b   c   d

e   f   g   h

Cover Photo: Robert Murase

Robert K. Murase
Pages 14, 15, 17, 19, 26fh, 30, 32bf,
39, 40, 41, 43e, 48, 49, 50, 51, 53d,
54dh, 56abdef, 58

Scott Murase
Pages 16, 18, 20, 21, 26eg, 28bef, 29,
32cdgh, 34, 35, 42, 43abf, 52, 53cgh

Timothy Hursley
Pages 10, 11b, 12, 23b, 24g

Bruce Forster
Pages 9, 13, 23aef

Greg Kozawa
Pages 4, 11ab, 25e

Steven Cridland
Pages 11ef, 24h, 25f

Lorraine Sako
Pages 44, 45, 54abef

Courtesy of Nishikawa Zoen
Pages 46, 47, 56h

Notes

1. Derek O. Ostergard, *George Nakashima: Full Circle* (New York: Weidenfeld & Nicolson, 1989).

2. J. William Thompson, "Stones on the Pacific Rim," *Landscape Architecture*, (March 1989).

3. Mark Hinshaw, "Making Waves on the Waterfront," *The Seattle Times* (July 23, 1995).

4. Doug Marx, "Zen and the Art of Landscape Architecture," *Northwest Magazine* (October 15, 1989).

5. J. William Thompson, "Stones on the Pacific Rim," *Landscape Architecture* (March 1989).

6. Ibid.

7. Benjamin Forgey, "Noguchi at Shikoku," *Landscape Architecture* (April 1990).

8. Sam Hunter, *Isamu Noguchi* (New York: Abbeville Press, 1978).

9. Joseph Esherick, letter to the American Institute of Architects nominating Japanese-American Historical Plaza for the 1996 Henry Bacon Medal (October 9, 1995).

10. Masayo Umezawa Duus, *Unlikely Liberators: The Men of the 100th and 442nd* (Honolulu: University of Hawaii Press, 1987).

11. Robert Landauer, "A Tribute Etched in Stone," *The Sunday Oregonian* (May 19, 1996).

12. Randy Gragg, "Memorial to Internment," *The Sunday Oregonian* (August 5, 1990).

13. Mark Holborn, *The Ocean in the Sand: Japan from Landscape to Garden* (Boulder, Colorado: Shambhala Publications, 1978).

14. William Howard Adams, *Nature Perfected: Gardens Through History* (New York: Abbeville Press, 1991).

15. Ibid.

16. Mark Holborn, *The Ocean in the Sand: Japan from Landscape to Garden* (Boulder, Colorado: Shambhala Publications, 1978).

17. Robert K. Murase, unpublished essay (Spring 1976).

18. "Myodo Kyo Kai: Honor Award," *Landscape Architecture* (September 1980).

19. Mark Holborn, *The Ocean in the Sand: Japan from Landscape to Garden* (Boulder, Colorado: Shambhala Publications, 1978).

20. Isamu Noguchi, letter to Robert Murase (July 8, 1977).

21. Ann Sullivan, "Memorial to Japanese-Americans Takes Shape," *The Oregonian* (July 25, 1990).

22. Robert K. Murase, "The Language of Stone," *Landscape Architecture* (November 1979).

23. Peter Staten, "Cannery Row," *Seattle Weekly* (September 24, 1993).

24. Carol Willis, *Form Follows Finance: Skyscraper and Skylines in New York and Chicago* (New York: Princeton Architectural Press, 1995).

25. Lee Geistlinger, "Sneaker War Spoils," *American Nurseryman* (December 1, 1994).

26. Zenkei Shibayama, *The Enso of Painting* (Tokyo: Sunjyu–sha, 1969).

27. Robert K. Murase, letter to Dina Ingerslev Nielsen and Hilary Adler Fenchel (June 27, 1991).

Bibliography

Carl Abbott, "Rivers in the City: Japanese-American Plaza," *Landscape Architecture* (February 1991).

William Howard Adams, *Nature Perfected: Gardens Through History* (New York: Abbeville Press, 1991).

Dore Ashton, "Space as Sculpture," *Landscape Architecture* (April 1990).

John Beardsley, "The Machine Becomes a Poem," *Landscape Architecture* (April 1990).

Ann Breen and Dick Rigby, *Waterfronts: Cities Reclaim Their Edge* (New York: McGraw-Hill, 1994).

Margaret Cottom-Winslow, *International Landscape Design: Architecture of Gardens, Parks & Open Spaces* (New York: PBC International, 1991).

Ian Cramb, *The Art of the Stonemason* (Crozet, Virginia: Betterway, 1992).

Masayo Umezawa Duus, *Unlikely Liberators: The Men of the 100th and 442nd* (Honolulu: University of Hawaii Press, 1987).

Joseph Esherick, letter to the American Institute of Architects nominating Japanese-American Historical Plaza for the 1996 Henry Bacon Medal (October 9, 1995).

Suzy Farbman, "Room with a View: Cool, Calm and Reflective," *Garden Design* (September, 1991).

Curtis P. Fields, *The Forgotten Art of Building a Stone Wall* (Dublin, New Hampshire: Yankee, 1971).

Benjamin Forgey, "Noguchi at Shikoku," *Landscape Architecture* (April 1990).

Lee Geistlinger, "Sneaker War Spoils," *American Nurseryman* (December 1, 1994).

Randy Gragg, "Memorial to Internment," *The Sunday Oregonian* (August 5, 1990).

Mark Hinshaw, "Making Waves on the Waterfront," *The Seattle Times* (July 23, 1995).

Mark Holborn, *The Ocean in the Sand: Japan from Landscape to Garden* (Boulder, Colorado: Shambhala Publications, 1978).

Sam Hunter, *Isamu Noguchi* (New York: Abbeville Press, 1978).

John Jerome, *Stone Work: Reflections on Serious Play and Other Aspects of Country Life* (New York: Penguin Books, 1989).

Jory Johnson, *Modern Landscape Architecture: Redefining the Garden* (New York: Abbeville Press, 1991).

Shuichi Kato, *Japan: Spirit & Form* (Rutland, Vermont and Tokyo: Charles E. Tuttle Company, 1994).

Jane Holtz Kay, "The Taj of Tone: Is Nike's Campus 'Green' or Just 'Greenwash,'" *Landscape Architecture* (June 1993).

Loraine Kuck, *The World of the Japanese Gardens: From Chinese Origins to Modern Landscape Art* (New York/Tokyo: Walker/Weatherhill, 1968).

Robert Landauer, "A Tribute Etched in Stone," *The Sunday Oregonian* (May 19, 1996).

Sutherland Lyall, *Designing the New Landscape* (New York: Van Nostrand Reinhold, 1993).

Doug Marx, "Zen and the Art of Landscape Architecture," *Northwest Magazine* (October 15, 1989).

Penelope Mason, *History of Japanese Art* (New York: Harry N. Abrams, 1993).

Robert K. Murase, unpublished essay (Spring 1976).

Robert K. Murase, "The Language of Stone," *Landscape Architecture* (November 1979).

Robert K. Murase, letter to Dina Ingerslev Nielsen and Hilary Adler Fenchel (June 27, 1991).

George Nakashima, *The Soul of a Tree: A Woodworker's Reflections* (Tokyo, New York and San Franscisco: Kodansha International Ltd., 1981).

Isamu Noguchi, letter to Robert Murase (July 8, 1977).

Derek O. Ostergard, *George Nakashima: Full Circle* (New York: Weidenfeld & Nicolson, 1989).

Masahiko Sato, *Arts of Japan 2: Kyoto Ceramics* (New York/Tokyo: Weatherhill/ Shibundo, 1973).

Mark Sherman and George Katagiri, editors, *Touching the Stones: Tracing One Hundred Years of Japanese-American History* (Portland: Oregon Nikkei Endowment, 1994).

Yoshiaki Shimizu, ed., *Japan: The Shaping of Daimyo Culture, 1185–1868* (New York: George Braziller, Inc., 1988).

Peter Staten, "Cannery Row," *Seattle Weekly* (September 24, 1993).

Harold P. Stern, *Birds, Beasts, Blossoms, and Bugs: The Nature of Japan* (New York: Harry N. Abrams, Inc., 1976).

J. William Thompson, "Stones on the Pacific Rim," *Landscape Architecture* (March 1989).

Peter Walker, "A Levitation of Stones," *Landscape Architecture* (April 1990).

Allen Wardell, "Prospect," *Landscape Architecture* (April 1990).

Carol Willis, *Form Follows Finance: Skyscraper and Skylines in New York and Chicago* (New York: Princeton Architectural Press, 1995).

Tom Wright and Mizuno Katsuhiko, *Zen Gardens: Kyoto's Nature Enclosed* (Kyoto: Suiko Books, 1990).

A student once asked Bob to explain "the language of rock." He responded: "Working with stones is a very intuitive art form where one's flow is spontaneous and direct. You engage a stone and find its face and decide its place in the landscape. Other stones follow to support and give balance to the emerging stone composition. As I'm sure you can understand, the feel for making a landscape is difficult. This feel cannot be measured or learned through books and can be drawn on a plan only to a limited extent. Read about historical styles and visit the gardens. I can only say that to learn by direct experience is your best way." [27]